Collins

easy le

Multiplication and division

quick quizzes

Ages 5–7

Trevor Dixon

Multiplication arrays

Write a number sentence for each array of dots.

Count the rows. Then count the dots in each row.

1    2 × 2 = ☐

2    ☐ × ☐ = ☐

3    ☐ × ☐ = ☐

4   ☐ × ☐ = ☐

Write two different number sentences for each array of dots.

5 • •

1 × 2 = ☐

2 × 1 = ☐

6 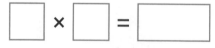   ☐ × ☐ = ☐

☐ × ☐ = ☐

7    ☐ × ☐ = ☐

☐ × ☐ = ☐

8 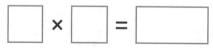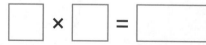   ☐ × ☐ = ☐

☐ × ☐ = ☐

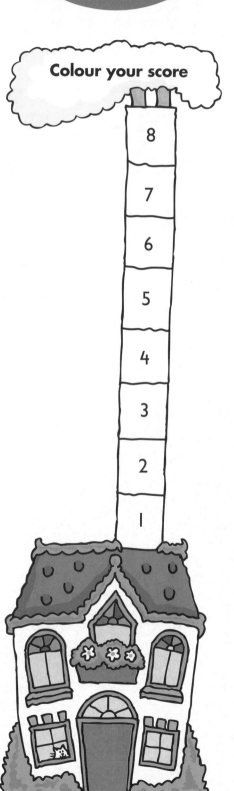

Colour your score

8

7

6

5

4

3

2

1

Arrays for division

Look at each array and write the answer to the question.

1. How many twos? ☐

2. How many twos? ☐

3. How many fives? ☐

4. How many threes? ☐

5. How many twos? ☐

6. How many twos? ☐

7. How many ones? ☐

8. How many threes? ☐

9. How many fours? ☐

10. How many threes? ☐

Count the number of rows or columns.

10

9

8

7

6

5

4

3

1

2

Colour your score

3

Repeated addition

Write the answers.

1 ●● + ●● + ●●
= 2 + 2 + 2 = 3 × 2 = ☐

Count the number of dots or pens in a set. Then count the sets.

2 ●● + ●● + ●● + ●●
= 2 + 2 + 2 + 2 = 4 × 2 = ☐

3 ●●●●● + ●●●●●
= 5 + 5 = 2 × 5 = ☐

4 ●● + ●● + ●● + ●● + ●●
= 2 + 2 + 2 + 2 + 2 = 5 × 2 = ☐

5 ●●●●● + ●●●●● + ●●●●●
= 5 + 5 + 5 = 3 × 5 = ☐

How many pens altogether?

6  ☐

7 ☐

8 ☐

9 ☐

10  ☐

Colour your score

4

Doubling

Write the answers.

 **ducks**

 **cats**

  **dogs**

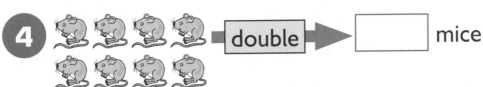 **mice**

 **ants**

Fill in the missing numbers.

6 ●●● 2 doubled is [ ]

7 [ ] doubled is 10
●●●●●●●●●●●

8 ●●●●●●●●●●●
10 doubled is [ ]

9 ●●●●● 4 doubled is [ ]

10 ●●●●●●●●●● 8 doubled is [ ]

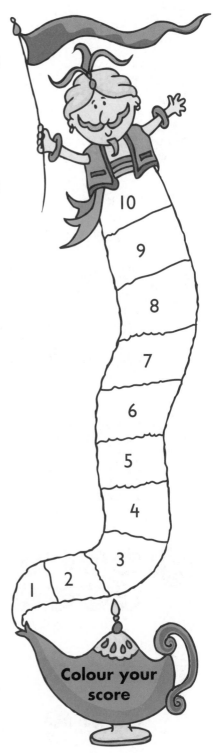

Doubling is multiplying by 2.

10
9
8
7
6
5
4
3
2
1

Colour your score

Grouping and sharing

Here are 12 stars.

How many stars in each group?

1 Divide the stars into 2 groups. ☐

2 Divide the stars into 6 groups. ☐

3 Divide the stars into 4 groups. ☐

4 Divide the stars into 3 groups. ☐

All the groups are equal when you share.

Share each set between two people.

How many does each person get?

5  → ☐ pennies

6  → ☐ pencils

7 → ☐ apples

8 → ☐ cupcakes

Colour your score

Halving

How many is half?

Draw a ring around half the set.

Write the answer.

Halving is dividing by 2.

1

2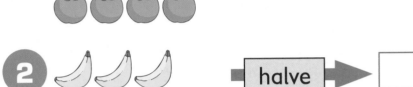

3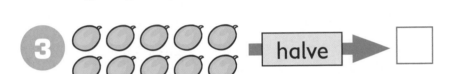

4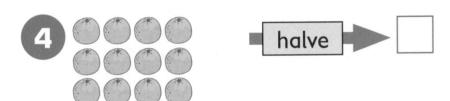

5

Halve each set.

Circle the answer.

6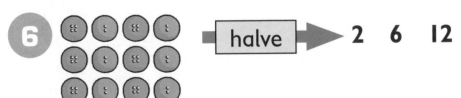

7

8

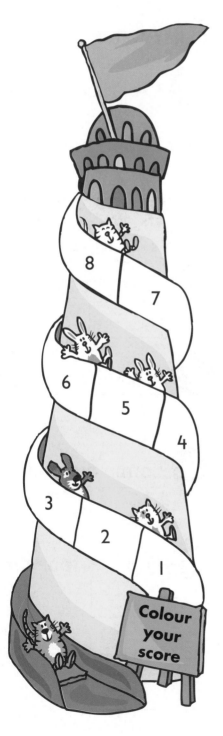

Colour your score

7

Counting groups

Work out how many objects each person has. Write your answer.

Count each group of objects the given number of times.

Jan has three pencils.

1 Tom has 2 times as many.

2 Sally has 5 times as many.

3 Ali has 10 times as many.

4 Obi has 4 times as many.

5 Poppy has 3 times as many.

Harry has five tennis balls.

6 Gary has two times as many.

7 Holly has five times as many.

8 Samir has ten times as many.

9 Mia has four times as many.

10 Kate has three times as many.

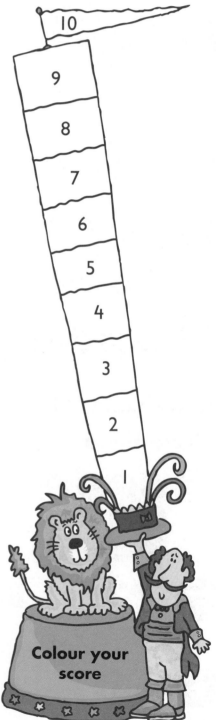

Colour your score

8

Making groups

How many objects are in each group?
Fill in the missing numbers.

Jay has ten sweets.

Draw rings around the objects to make groups if it helps.

1 Jay puts them into 5 groups of ☐.

2 Jay puts them into 10 groups of ☐.

Jenny has eight cupcakes.

3 Jenny puts them into 2 groups of ☐.

4 Jenny puts them into 4 groups of ☐.

5 Jenny puts them into 8 groups of ☐.

6 Jenny puts them into 1 group of ☐.

Ari has six apples.

7 Ari puts them into 2 groups of ☐.

8 Ari puts them into 6 groups of ☐.

9 Ari puts them into 3 groups of ☐.

10 Ari puts them into 1 group of ☐.

Colour your score

10
9
8
7
6
5
4
3
2
1

2 times table

Draw a line from each multiplication to the correct answer.

Count up in twos if you need to.

1 | 2 × 2   12

2 | 4 × 2   4

3 | 5 × 2   10

4 | 7 × 2   8

5 | 6 × 2   14

Choose the correct number to complete each multiplication fact.

16 20 6 22 18 2 24 0

6 3 × 2 = ☐

7 10 × 2 = ☐

8 9 × 2 = ☐

9 11 × 2 = ☐

10 8 × 2 = ☐

11 0 × 2 = ☐

12 12 × 2 = ☐

13 1 × 2 = ☐

14 2 × 3 = ☐

15 2 × 10 = ☐

Colour your score

15
14
13
12
11
10
9
8
7
6
5
4
3
2
1

Division facts: ÷ 2

Draw a line from each division to the correct answer.

1 | 6 ÷ 2   5

2 | 10 ÷ 2   1

3 | 2 ÷ 2   3

4 | 4 ÷ 2   0

5 | 0 ÷ 2   2

If you know 3 × 2 = 6, then you know 6 ÷ 2 = 3.

Write the answers.

6 8 ÷ 2 =

7 12 ÷ 2 =

8 16 ÷ 2 =

9 20 ÷ 2 =

10 14 ÷ 2 =

11 10 ÷ 2 =

12 24 ÷ 2 =

13 22 ÷ 2 =

14 18 ÷ 2 =

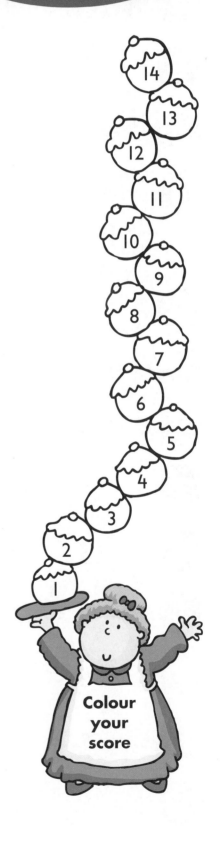

Colour your score

5 times table

Each hand has five fingers.

Write a number sentence for each set of hands.

All the answers end in 5 or 0.

1 4 × 5 = ☐

2 ☐ × 5 = ☐

3 ☐ × ☐ = ☐

4 ☐ × ☐ = ☐

5 ☐ × ☐ = ☐

Circle the correct answer.

6 6 × 5 = **30   35   40**

7 0 × 5 = **0   1   5**

8 8 × 5 = **30   40   50**

9 7 × 5 = **75   40   35**

10 12 × 5 = **50   60   70**

11 9 × 5 = **45   40   90**

12 10 × 5 = **15   50   105**

Colour your score

12

Division facts: ÷ 5

Put each number into the function machine and write the number that will come out.

If you know 4 × 5 = 20, then you know 20 ÷ 5 = 4.

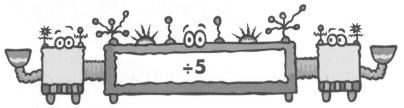

1. 10 → ÷5 → [ ]

2. 0 → ÷5 → [ ]

3. 15 → ÷5 → [ ]

4. 5 → ÷5 → [ ]

5. 25 → ÷5 → [ ]

6. 40 → ÷5 → [ ]

7. 45 → ÷5 → [ ]

8. 35 → ÷5 → [ ]

9. 55 → ÷5 → [ ]

10. 30 → ÷5 → [ ]

11. 20 → ÷5 → [ ]

12. 60 → ÷5 → [ ]

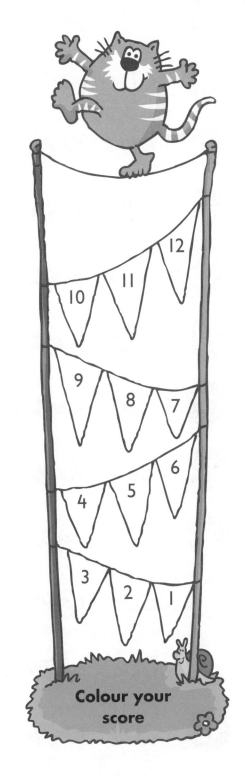

Colour your score

10 times table

£10

Count up in tens if you can't remember the times table.

Work out the total cost.

1 2 CDs ➡ £ ☐

2 9 CDs ➡ £ ☐

3 7 CDs ➡ £ ☐

4 10 CDs ➡ £ ☐

5 12 CDs ➡ £ ☐

6 11 CDs ➡ £ ☐

7 8 CDs ➡ £ ☐

8 1 CD ➡ £ ☐

9 3 CDs ➡ £ ☐

10 5 CDs ➡ £ ☐

11 4 CDs ➡ £ ☐

12 6 CDs ➡ £ ☐

Colour your score

Division facts: ÷ 10

Use each set of numbers to write
a division fact.

1 3, 10, 30

[   ] ÷ [   ] = [   ]

2 5, 10, 50

[   ] ÷ [   ] = [   ]

3 4, 40, 10

[   ] ÷ [   ] = [   ]

4 90, 10, 9

[   ] ÷ [   ] = [   ]

5 10, 6, 60

[   ] ÷ [   ] = [   ]

6 10, 1, 10

[   ] ÷ [   ] = [   ]

7 11, 110, 10

[   ] ÷ [   ] = [   ]

8 0, 0, 10

[   ] ÷ [   ] = [   ]

9 70, 10, 7

[   ] ÷ [   ] = [   ]

10 80, 10, 8

[   ] ÷ [   ] = [   ]

Start with the largest number.

9
10
8
7
6
5
4
3
2
1

Colour
your score

Mixed times tables

Work out the total amount in pence.

Count up in twos, fives or tens if you need to.

1  → [ ] p

2  → [ ] p

3  → [ ] p

4 → [ ] p

5  → [ ] p

6 9 ×  → [ ] p

7 11 ×  → [ ] p

8 7 ×  → [ ] p

9 12 ×  → [ ] p

10 8 ×  → [ ] p

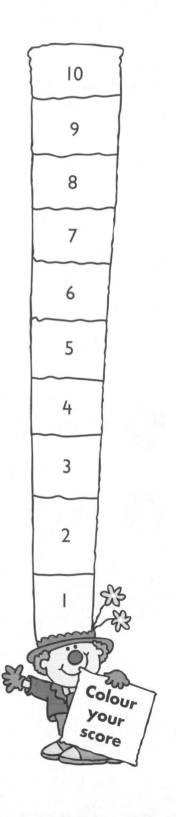

Colour your score

10
9
8
7
6
5
4
3
2
1

16

Mixed division facts

Put a tick if the answer is 8.
If not, put a cross.

1 70 ÷ 10 ☐

2 14 ÷ 2 ☐

3 40 ÷ 5 ☐

4 10 ÷ 2 ☐

5 16 ÷ 2 ☐

Use your times tables facts, e.g. how many tens make 70?

Tom has got the answers to these division facts muddled up.

Write the correct answers.

6 55 ÷ 5 = [3] ✗ 55 ÷ 5 = [   ]

7 90 ÷ 10 = [1] ✗ 90 ÷ 10 = [   ]

8 24 ÷ 2 = [11] ✗ 24 ÷ 2 = [   ]

9 30 ÷ 10 = [12] ✗ 30 ÷ 10 = [   ]

10 5 ÷ 5 = [9] ✗ 5 ÷ 5 = [   ]

11 50 ÷ 10 = [4] ✗ 50 ÷ 10 = [   ]

12 20 ÷ 5 = [5] ✗ 20 ÷ 5 = [   ]

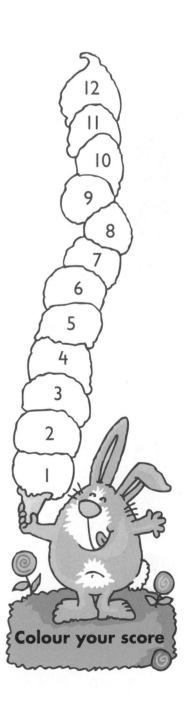

12
11
10
9
8
7
6
5
4
3
2
1

Colour your score

Missing numbers

Fill in the missing numbers.

Use your times tables facts, e.g. 4 times what makes 20?

1   4   ×   ☐   =   20

2   ☐   ×   2   =   6

3   10   ×   ☐   =   80

4   ☐   ×   5   =   35

5   2   ×   ☐   =   18

6   ☐   ×   10   =   120

7   5   ×   ☐   =   50

8   ☐   ×   2   =   16

9   10   ×   ☐   =   70

10   ☐   ×   2   =   14

11   2   ×   ☐   =   22

12   ☐   ×   10   =   100

13   5   ×   ☐   =   40

14   ☐   ×   10   =   60

15   2   ×   ☐   =   0

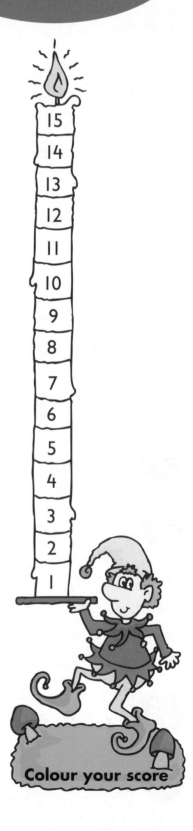

Colour your score

More missing numbers

Fill in the missing number.

1 ☐ ÷ 2 = 4

2 60 ÷ ☐ = 10

3 ☐ ÷ 5 = 3

4 12 ÷ ☐ = 2

5 ☐ ÷ 10 = 10

6 16 ÷ ☐ = 2

7 ☐ ÷ 5 = 7

8 50 ÷ ☐ = 5

9 ☐ ÷ 5 = 6

10 22 ÷ ☐ = 2

11 ☐ ÷ 5 = 9

12 40 ÷ ☐ = 4

13 ☐ ÷ 5 = 10

14 24 ÷ ☐ = 2

15 ☐ ÷ 10 = 0

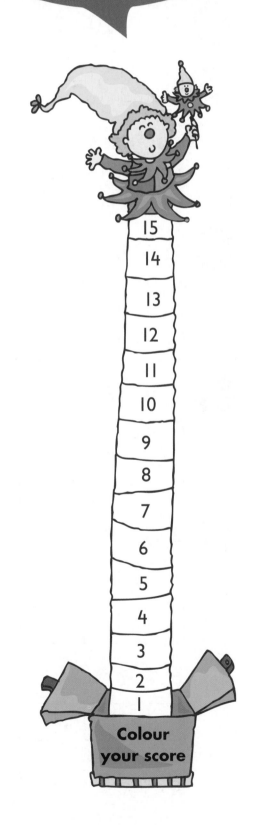

You need to know your times tables to get these right!

15
14
13
12
11
10
9
8
7
6
5
4
3
2
1

Colour your score

Working with 2

Write ×, ÷ or = to complete each number sentence.

1 4 ☐ 2 = 8

2 10 ☐ 20 ÷ 2

3 18 ☐ 2 = 9

4 16 ☐ 8 ☐ 2

5 6 ☐ 2 ☐ 3

6 22 ☐ 2 ☐ 11

Use the facts you know about multiplying and dividing by 2.

Use each set of numbers to write two multiplication facts and two division facts.

7 2, 4, 8

2 × 4 = ☐   4 × 2 = ☐
8 ÷ 2 = ☐   8 ÷ 4 = ☐

8 2, 8, 16

☐ × ☐ = ☐   ☐ × ☐ = ☐
☐ ÷ ☐ = ☐   ☐ ÷ ☐ = ☐

9 2, 5, 10

☐ × ☐ = ☐   ☐ × ☐ = ☐
☐ ÷ ☐ = ☐   ☐ ÷ ☐ = ☐

10 1, 2, 2

☐ × ☐ = ☐   ☐ × ☐ = ☐
☐ ÷ ☐ = ☐   ☐ ÷ ☐ = ☐

10 9 8 7 6 5 4 3 2 1

Colour your score

20

More working with 2

Circle all the numbers that are answers in the two times table.

1   4   7   10   13   22

2   9   14   18   21   24

3   3   17   20   26   40

4   8   11   12   15   28

5   1   5   16   30   31

All even numbers are answers in the two times table.

This function machine doubles numbers.

double

Write the missing numbers.

6   5   → double →   [ ]

7   [ ]   → double →   8

8   11   → double →   [ ]

9   [ ]   → double →   30

10   20   → double →   [ ]

Colour your score

21

Working with 5

Write ×, ÷ or = to complete each number sentence.

 1 5 ☐ 5 = 25

4 11 ☐ 5 ☐ 55

2 4 = 20 ☐ 5

5 30 ☐ 5 ☐ 6

3 12 = 60 ☐ 5

Use the facts you know about multiplying and dividing by 5.

The numbers on a clock are 5 minutes apart.

For each clock, write down how many minutes it is past the hour.

6  ☐ minutes past

7  ☐ minutes past

8  ☐ minutes past

9  ☐ minutes past

10  ☐ minutes past

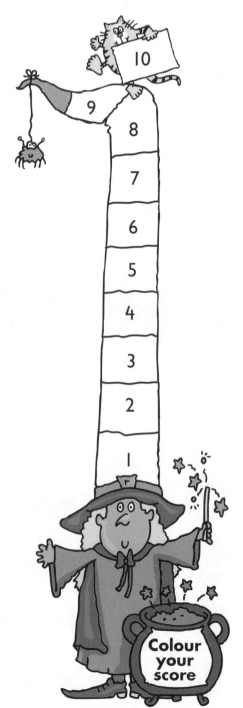

Colour your score

More working with 5

Fill in the missing multiples of 5.

1   30   [ ]   40   45   50

2   45   50   55   60   [ ]

3   [ ]   10   15   20   25

4   35   30   [ ]   20   15

5   50   45   40   35   [ ]

All the multiples of five end in 5 or 0.

Circle all the multiples of 5.

Write a multiplication fact for each multiple you find.

7	15	23	30
17	28	41	35
45	52	13	19
37	24	60	53

6   [ ]   × 5 =   [ ]

7   [ ]   × 5 =   [ ]

8   [ ]   × 5 =   [ ]

9   [ ]   × 5 =   [ ]

10   [ ]   × 5 =   [ ]

Colour your score

10 9 8 7 6 5 4 3 2 1

23

Working with 10

Write ×, ÷ or = to complete each number sentence.

Use the facts you know about multiplying and dividing by 10.

1 40 ☐ 10 = 4

2 6 ☐ 60 ÷ 10

3 30 ☐ 10 ☐ 3

4 8 ☐ 80 ☐ 10

5 12 ☐ 10 ☐ 120

Complete the place value cards.
One has been done for you.

| 4 ones | × 10 = | 4 tens |

6 | 5 ones | × 10 = | ___ tens |

7 | ___ ones | × 10 = | 6 tens |

8 | 8 ones | × 10 = | ___ tens |

9 | 3 ones | × 10 = | ___ tens |

10 | ___ ones | × 10 = | 9 tens |

10 9 8 7 6 5 4 3 2 1

Colour your score

24

More working with 10

This function machine divides by 10.

To find a missing input, multiply the output by 10.

Fill in the missing numbers.

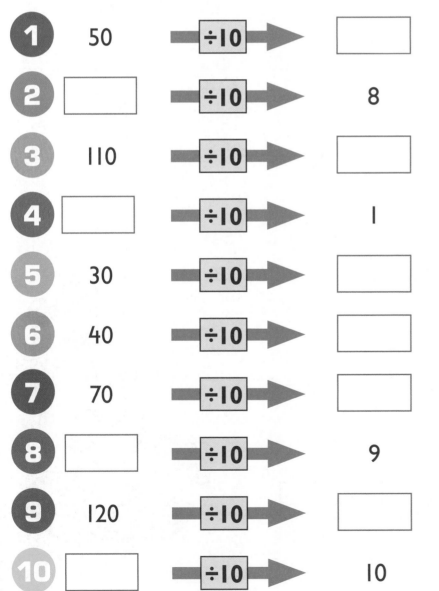

1 50 ÷10 → ▢

2 ▢ ÷10 → 8

3 110 ÷10 → ▢

4 ▢ ÷10 → 1

5 30 ÷10 → ▢

6 40 ÷10 → ▢

7 70 ÷10 → ▢

8 ▢ ÷10 → 9

9 120 ÷10 → ▢

10 ▢ ÷10 → 10

Colour your score

Multiplication problems

Fill in the missing numbers.

1 4 + 4 + 4 + 4 + 4
= 5 × ☐ = ☐

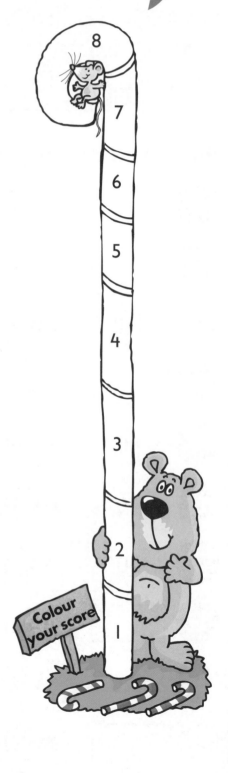

> Turn the multiplication around if it helps, e.g. 5 × 4 = 4 × 5.

2 🍊🍊🍊 + 🍊🍊🍊
= 2 × ☐ = ☐

3 6 + 6 + 6 + 6 + 6 + 6 + 6 + 6 + 6 + 6
= ☐ × 6 = ☐

4 🍎🍎🍎🍎🍎 🍎🍎🍎🍎🍎 🍎🍎🍎🍎🍎 = 3 × ☐ = ☐

5 10 + 10 + 10 + 10 + 10 + 10 + 10
= ☐ × 10 = ☐

6 12 + 12 + 12 + 12 + 12
= ☐ × 12 = ☐

7 2 + 2 + 2 + 2 + 2 + 2 + 2 + 2 + 2 + 2
= 10 × ☐ = ☐

8 🍓🍓🍓🍓🍓 🍓🍓🍓🍓🍓 = 5 × ☐ = ☐

Colour your score

26

Problem-solving

Write the total amount.

1 Two £5 notes  £ [ ]

2 Seven 5 p coins ➤ [ ] p

Count up in twos, fives or tens if you need to.

3 Three £10 notes ➤ £ [ ]

4 Eight 10 p coins ➤ [ ] p

5 Twelve 2 p coins ➤ [ ] p

6 Five bags with 10 sweets in each
➤ [ ] sweets

7 Seven bags with 2 sweets in each
➤ [ ] sweets

8 Eight bags with 5 sweets in each
➤ [ ] sweets

9 Nine bags with 5 sweets in each
➤ [ ] sweets

10 Seven bags with 10 sweets in each
➤ [ ] sweets

11 Four jugs holding 5 litres each
➤ [ ] litres

12 Ten jugs holding 10 litres each
➤ [ ] litres

Colour your score

Division problems

Write how many counters are in each group or share.

Here are 6 counters.

Use the pictures to help you.

1 Share the counters between 2 people.

➡ ☐ counters each

2 Divide the counters into 6 groups.

➡ ☐ counter each

3 Share the counters between 3 people.

➡ ☐ counters each

Here are 20 counters.

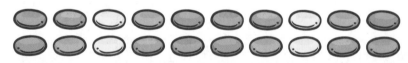

4 Share the counters between 10 people.

➡ ☐ counters each

5 Divide the counters into 2 groups.

➡ ☐ counters each

6 Share the counters between 4 people.

➡ ☐ counters each

7 Divide the counters into 5 groups.

➡ ☐ counters each

8 Share the counters between 20 people.

➡ ☐ counter each

More division problems

Write the answers.

1 Ben has 90 p in 10 p coins.
How many coins does he have?

☐ coins

2 Kim shares £100 between 10 people.
How much does each person have?

£ ☐

3 There are 16 biscuits in a box.
Dev puts half of them on a plate.
How many biscuits are on the plate?

☐ biscuits

4 Amy has 30 litres of juice.
She puts the juice into 5 litre jugs.
How many jugs does she need?

☐ jugs

5 Saskia has 45 bananas.
She shares them between 5 bowls.
How many bananas are in each bowl?

☐ bananas

6 Max has 60 kg of sugar.
How many 10 kg bags could he fill?

☐ bags

Divide the larger number by the smaller number.

Colour your score

Commutativity

Put a tick if the number sentence is correct.

If not, put a cross.

1   4 × 5 = 5 × 4 ☐

2   10 ÷ 2 = 2 ÷ 10 ☐

3   30 ÷ 10 = 10 ÷ 30 ☐

4   16 ÷ 2 = 2 ÷ 16 ☐

5   2 × 5 = 5 × 2 ☐

6   12 ÷ 2 = 2 ÷ 12 ☐

7   3 × 10 = 10 × 3 ☐

8   9 × 5 = 5 × 9 ☐

9   60 ÷ 10 = 10 ÷ 60 ☐

10   7 × 5 = 5 × 7 ☐

11   8 × 2 = 2 × 8 ☐

12   90 ÷ 10 = 10 ÷ 90 ☐

13   25 ÷ 5 = 5 ÷ 25 ☐

14   10 × 10 = 10 × 10 ☐

15   10 ÷ 10 = 10 ÷ 10 ☐

Multiplication of two numbers can be done in any order (it is commutative), but division cannot.

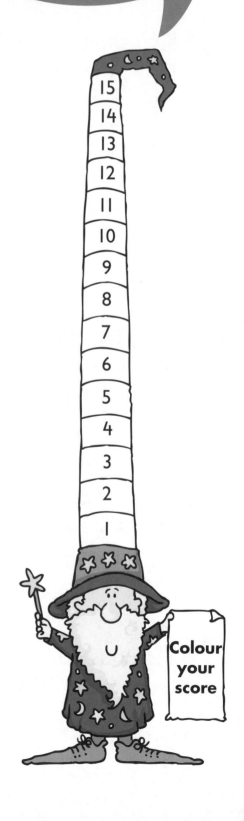

15
14
13
12
11
10
9
8
7
6
5
4
3
2
1

Colour your score

Checking answers

Complete the inverse calculations.

1 $6 \times 5 = 30$ $30 \div 5 = \boxed{}$

2 $24 \div 2 = 12$ $12 \times 2 = \boxed{}$

3 $7 \times 10 = 70$ $70 \div 10 = \boxed{}$

4 $15 \div 5 = 3$ $3 \times 5 = \boxed{}$

5 $120 \div 10 = 12$ $12 \times 10 = \boxed{}$

> **Inverse means opposite. Dividing and multiplying are opposites.**

Write the inverse calculation to check each answer.

Put a tick if it is correct.
If not, put a cross.

6 $60 \div 5 = 12$ $\boxed{}$

$\boxed{} \times \boxed{} = \boxed{}$

7 $8 \times 10 = 80$ $\boxed{}$

$\boxed{} \div \boxed{} = \boxed{}$

8 $7 \times 5 = 45$ $\boxed{}$

$\boxed{} \div \boxed{} = \boxed{}$

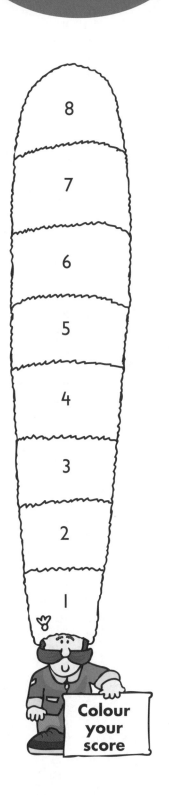

8
7
6
5
4
3
2
1

Colour your score

Answers

Multiplication arrays
1. 4
2. $3 \times 3 = 9$
3. $4 \times 4 = 16$
4. $5 \times 5 = 25$
5. $1 \times 2 = 2, 2 \times 1 = 2$
6. $3 \times 5 = 15, 5 \times 3 = 15$
7. $2 \times 7 = 14, 7 \times 2 = 14$
8. $4 \times 2 = 8, 2 \times 4 = 8$

Arrays for division
1. 2
2. 3
3. 2
4. 2
5. 5
6. 4
7. 2
8. 5
9. 2
10. 3

Repeated addition
1. 6
2. 8
3. 10
4. 10
5. 15
6. 6
7. 10
8. 8
9. 12
10. 25

Doubling
1. 6
2. 8
3. 10
4. 16
5. 4
6. 4
7. 5
8. 20
9. 8
10. 16

Grouping and sharing
1. 6
2. 2
3. 3
4. 4
5. 6 pennies
6. 5 pencils
7. 4 apples
8. 3 cupcakes

Halving
1. 4
2. 3
3. 5
4. 6
5. 2
6. 6
7. 2
8. 1

Counting groups
1. 6
2. 15
3. 30
4. 12
5. 9
6. 10
7. 25
8. 50
9. 20
10. 15

Making groups
1. 2
2. 1
3. 4
4. 2
5. 1
6. 8

7. 3
8. 1

9. 2
10. 6

2 times table
1. 4
2. 8
3. 10
4. 14
5. 12
6. 6
7. 20
8. 18
9. 22
10. 16
11. 0
12. 24
13. 2
14. 6
15. 20

Division facts: ÷ 2
1. 3
2. 5
3. 1
4. 2
5. 0
6. 4
7. 6
8. 8
9. 10
10. 7
11. 5
12. 12
13. 11
14. 9

5 times table
1. 20
2. 2, 10
3. $3 \times 5 = 15$
4. $5 \times 5 = 25$
5. $1 \times 5 = 5$
6. 30
7. 0
8. 40
9. 35
10. 60
11. 45
12. 50

Division facts: ÷ 5
1. 2
2. 0
3. 3
4. 1
5. 5
6. 8
7. 9
8. 7
9. 11
10. 6
11. 4
12. 12

10 times table
1. £20
2. £90
3. £70
4. £100
5. £120
6. £110
7. £80
8. £10
9. £30
10. £50
11. £40
12. £60

Division facts: ÷ 10
1. $30 \div 10 = 3 / 30 \div 3 = 10$
2. $50 \div 10 = 5 / 50 \div 5 = 10$
3. $40 \div 10 = 4 / 40 \div 4 = 10$
4. $90 \div 10 = 9 / 90 \div 9 = 10$
5. $60 \div 10 = 6 / 60 \div 6 = 10$
6. $10 \div 10 = 1$
7. $110 \div 10 = 11 / 110 \div 11 = 10$
8. $0 \div 10 = 0$
9. $70 \div 10 = 7 / 70 \div 7 = 10$
10. $80 \div 10 = 8 / 80 \div 8 = 10$

Mixed times tables
1. 25 p
2. 60 p
3. 8 p
4. 30 p
5. 40 p
6. 18 p
7. 55 p
8. 70 p
9. 60 p
10. 16 p

Mixed division facts
1. ✗
2. ✗
3. ✓
4. ✗
5. ✓
6. 11
7. 9
8. 12
9. 3
10. 1
11. 5
12. 4

Missing numbers
1. 5
2. 3
3. 8
4. 7
5. 9
6. 12
7. 10
8. 8
9. 7
10. 7
11. 11
12. 10
13. 8
14. 6
15. 0

More missing numbers
1. 8
2. 6
3. 15
4. 6
5. 100
6. 8
7. 35
8. 10
9. 30
10. 11
11. 45
12. 10
13. 50
14. 12
15. 0

Working with 2
1. ×
2. =
3. ÷
4. ÷ = / = ×
5. ÷ = / = ×
6. ÷ = / = ×
7. $2 \times 4 = 8, 4 \times 2 = 8, 8 \div 4 = 2, 8 \div 2 = 4$
8. $2 \times 8 = 16, 8 \times 2 = 16, 16 \div 2 = 8, 16 \div 8 = 2$
9. $2 \times 5 = 10, 5 \times 2 = 10, 10 \div 2 = 5, 10 \div 5 = 2$
10. $1 \times 2 = 2, 2 \times 1 = 2, 2 \div 2 = 1, 2 \div 1 = 2$